Bag Lunches

kids cook!

KIDS COOK SERIES

Canadian Cataloguing in Publication Data

Main entry under title:

Kids cook bag lunches

(Kids cook series)
Recipes selected from the Company's Coming cookbooks.
Includes index.
Co-published by The Recipe Factory Inc.
ISBN 1-896891-43-8

1. Lunchbox cookery—Juvenile literature. I. Recipe Factory Inc.
II. Title: Bag lunches. III. Series.
TX735.K53 2000   j641.5'3   C00-900408-4

Published by
Company's Coming Publishing Limited
2311 - 96 Street
Edmonton, Alberta, Canada T6N 1G3
www.companyscoming.com

Printed In China

Table of Contents

Company's Coming Cookbooks

Original Series

- 150 Delicious Squares
- Casseroles
- Muffins & More
- Salads
- Appetizers
- Desserts
- Soups & Sandwiches
- Cookies
- Pasta
- Barbecues
- Light Recipes
- Preserves

- Chicken
- Kids Cooking
- Cooking For Two
- Breakfasts & Brunches
- Slow Cooker Recipes
- One-Dish Meals
- Starters
- Stir-Fry
- Make-Ahead Meals
- The Potato Book
- Low-Fat Cooking
- Low-Fat Pasta

- Cook For Kids
- Stews, Chilies & Chowders
- Fondues
- The Beef Book
- Asian Cooking
- The Cheese Book
- The Rookie Cook
- Rush-Hour Recipes
- Sweet Cravings **NEW**
  November 1/02

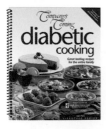

Greatest Hits Series

- Italian
- Mexican

Lifestyle Series

- Grilling
- Diabetic Cooking

Special Occasion Series

- Gifts from the Kitchen
- Cooking for the Seasons
- Home for the Holidays **NEW** *October 1/02*

Foreword

Tired of the same-old, same-old in your lunch bag? Take matters into your own hands and create the kind of lunch you really want! Included are some great recipes designed just for you such as wraps, dips, main course lunches and even sweet treats to complete your meal—all specially selected from the Company's Coming family of cookbooks. The Mix & Match Bag Lunch Suggestions on pages 10 and 11 will help you put together a tasty lunch that will be the envy of your classmates.

Before you get started, check out the Get Ready section of each recipe. Every utensil and piece of equipment you will need is listed in the order you will use it. Line them up as listed and you will have what you need when you need it! A picture dictionary of all the equipment and utensils can be found on pages 8 and 9. Any Cooking Terms you might not know are explained on pages 6 and 7.

Remember, there is always one important last step—clean up when you are finished, both at home when making your lunch, and at school after eating it.

Safety

1. Never touch anything electrical with your wet hands.
2. Always pull out a plug by holding and pulling on the plug itself, not the cord.
3. Keep saucepan handles turned inward on top of the stove.
4. Know how to properly use all appliances before starting. (Ask Mom or Dad if you're not sure.)
5. Handle hot plates and dishes with well-insulated oven mitts.
6. Turn off burners and oven, and unplug small appliances when not in use.

A note to parents: This book is intended for your children to use. It has been especially written for kids aged 8 to 15 years. Please supervise them when necessary. The handling of sharp knives, boiling liquids, and hot pans needs to be monitored carefully with younger children.

 # Cooking Terms

Bake
To cook in an oven preheated to the temperature it says in the recipe. Use either the bottom or center rack.

Batter
A mixture of flour, liquid and other ingredients that can be thin (such as pancake batter) or thick (such as muffin batter).

Beat
To mix two or more ingredients with a spoon, fork or electric mixer, using a circular motion.

Blend
To mix two or more ingredients with a spoon, fork, electric mixer, or electric blender until combined.

Boil
To heat a liquid in a saucepan until bubbles rise in a steady pattern and break on the surface. Steam also starts to rise from the surface.

Break An Egg
Tap the side of an egg on the edge of a bowl or cup to crack the shell. Place the tips of both thumbs in the crack and open the shell, letting the egg yolk and egg white drop into the bowl.

Broil
To cook under the top heating element in the oven. Use either the top rack or the upper rack.

Chill
To place in the refrigerator until cold.

Chop
To cut food into small pieces with a sharp knife on a cutting board; to chop finely is to cut foods as small as you can.

Combine
To put two or more ingredients together.

Cream
To beat an ingredient or combination of ingredients until the mixture is soft, smooth and "creamy," using a spoon or electric mixer.

Cut In
To combine butter or margarine with dry ingredients (such as flour) using a fork or pastry blender until the mixture looks like big crumbs the size of green peas.

Dice
To cut food into small ¼ inch (6 mm) cube-shaped pieces.

Drain
To strain away an unwanted liquid (such as water, fruit juice, or grease) using a colander or strainer. Drain water or juice over the kitchen sink or in a bowl. Drain grease into a metal can, chill until hardened, then throw away in the garbage.

Drizzle
To dribble drops or lines of glaze or icing over food in a random manner from tines of a fork or the tip of a spoon.

6

Fold

To mix gently, using a rubber spatula, by cutting down in the center and lifting towards the edge of the bowl. Use a "down, up, over" movement, turning the bowl as you repeat.

Garnish

To decorate food with edible condiments such as parsley sprigs, fruit slices or vegetable cut-outs.

Heat

To make something warm or hot by placing the saucepan on the stove burner that is turned on to the level it says in the recipe.

Knead

To work dough into a smooth putty-like mass by pressing and folding using the heels of your hands.

Let Stand

To let a baked product cool slightly on a wire rack or hot pad, while still in its baking pan. Also, any other mixture that requires time to sit on the counter for the flavors to blend.

Mash

To squash cooked or very ripe foods with a fork or potato masher.

Melt

To heat a solid food such as butter, margarine, cheese or chocolate, until it turns into a liquid. Be careful not to burn it.

Mix

(see Combine)

Mixing Just Until Moistened

To stir dry ingredients with liquid ingredients until dry ingredients are barely wet. Mixture will still be lumpy.

Process

To mix or cut up food in a blender (or food processor) until it is the way it says in the recipe.

Sauté

To cook food quickly in a small amount of oil in a frying pan, wok, or special sauté pan over medium heat.

Scramble-Fry

To brown ground meat in hot oil using a spoon, fork or pancake lifter to break up the meat into small crumb-like pieces as it cooks.

Scrape (Scraping down the sides)

To use a rubber spatula to remove as much of a mixture as possible from inside a bowl or saucepan.

Simmer

To heat liquids in a saucepan on low on the stove burner so that small bubbles appear on the surface around the sides of the liquid.

Slice

To cut foods such as apples, carrots, tomatoes, meat or bread into thin sections or pieces, using a sharp knife.

Spoon (into)

Using a spoon to scoop ingredients from one container to another.

Spread

To cover the surface of one product (generally a more solid food such as bread) with another product (generally a softer food such as icing or butter).

Stir

To mix two or more ingredients with a spoon, using a circular motion.

Stir-Fry

To heat food quickly in a frying pan on medium-high stirring constantly.

Toast

To brown slightly in a toaster, frying pan or under the broiler in the oven.

Toss

To mix salad or other ingredients gently with a lifting motion, using two forks, two spoons or salad tongs.

Equipment & Utensils

Barbecue fork

Blender

Baking sheet

Bread knife

Casserole dish

Cookie sheet

Colander

Cutting board

Dry measures

Frying pan

Electric mixer

Electric frying pan

Hot pad

Ice-cream scoop

Liquid measures

Mixing spoons

Measuring spoons

Loaf pan

Muffin pan

Bowls (mixing)

Oblong baking dish

Oblong baking pan

Oven mitts

Parfait spoon

Pancake lifter

Pastry brush

Pastry blender

Pie plate

Pizza pan

Rubber spatula

Rolling pin

Potato masher

Round cake pan

Square baking pan

Saucepan

Sharp knife

Table knife, fork & spoon

Tube pan

Sieve or strainer

Burners

Top Rack

Center Rack

Upper Rack

Bottom Rack

Oven with rack positions

Wire rack

Tongs

Whisk

9

Mix & Match
Bag Lunch Suggestions

BREADS	FRUIT	VEGETABLES
Bagels	Apricot Logs*	Raisins
Breadsticks	Banana Raisin Bars*	Bean & Tomato Salad*

Buns:
    Dinner
    Hamburger
    Hot Dog
    Kaiser
    Submarine
	Dried Fruit
	
	Fresh Fruit:
	    Apple
	    Banana
	    Blueberries
		Cottage Cheese Salad*
		
		Crunchy Potato Salad*
		
		Cucumber & Pea Salad*
		
		Cucumber Under Wraps*

English Muffins	Cantaloupe Grapefruit Sections	Fresh Vegetables: Asparagus

Loaves:
    Cheese
    Enriched Whites
    100% Whole Wheat
    Raisin
    Rye
    7-Grain
    60% Whole Wheat
	Grapes
	Kiwifruit
	Melon
	Nectarine
	Orange
	Peach
	Pear
	Plums
	Raspberries
	Strawberries
		Broccoli
		Carrot Sticks
		Cauliflower
		Celery Sticks
		Cherry Tomatoes
		Cucumber
		Green Beans
		Lettuce
		Radishes
		Tomatoes

Melba Toast		Zucchini

Muffins:
    Apple Granola*
    Date & Nut*
	Frozen Bananas*
	
	Frozen Grapes*
		Rice Salad*

Pepper Cheese Roll*	Frozen Oranges*	Salad Lunch*
Pita Bread Pickly Pita Pockets*	Fruit Juice	Tomato & Mozza Salad*
Soft Pretzel	Fruit Salad*	Tortellini Salad*

Tortillas:
    Peanut Butter Wrap*
    "Wurst" Cheese &
       Lettuce Wrap*
		Vegetable Juice
		
		Vegetable Roll*

* Recipe is included in this book. See Index for page number.

MILK & DAIRY	MEATS	EXTRAS

MILK & DAIRY

Cheese Slices:
  Cheddar
  Gouda
  Mozzarella

Cottage Cheese

Dips:
  Caesar*
  Garlic Mustard*
  Honey Mustard*
  Stick*

Macaroni & Cottage Cheese*

Milk:
  Homogenized
  2%
  1%
  Skim
  Chocolate

Yogurt (Plain or Fruit)

MEATS

Cold Cooked Chicken/Turkey

Crispy Chicken Cracky*

Ham & Melon Kabobs*

Hamburger*

Hard-boiled Egg

Hero Sandwich*

Muffuletta*

Quick Turkey Loaf*

Roast Beef Rolls*

Sandwich Fillings:
  Baked Bean*
  Beef*
  Cheese*
  Cheese & Lettuce*
  Cheese & Tomato*
  Chicken*
  Egg
  Ham & Cheese*
  Ham & Cuke*
  Ham & Lettuce*
  Ham & Tomato*
  Peanut Butter*
  Peanut Butter & Pickle*
  Peanut Butter Banana*
  Salmon
  Tuna*
  Turkey

Super Sausage Sub*

Tuna Biscuits*

Tuna Buns*

EXTRAS

Cookies:
  Butterscotch Pudding*
  Carrot*
  Corn Flakes Macaroons*
  Easy Raisin*
  Ginger Crinkles*
  Lemonade*
  Rolled Ginger*
  Snap Gingers*

Fruit Drink

Hot Dog*

Muffins:
  Lemon Blueberry*
  Orange Cranberry*

Pepper-Corn Crackers*

Snacks:
  Candied Popcorn*
  Citrus Crunchies*
  Corn Flakes Chews*
  Peanut Butter Popcorn
    Treats*
  Spiced Nuts*
  Summertime Snack Mix*
  Toasted Granola*
  Trail Mix

Squares:
  Butterscotch Bites*
  Chocolate Chip
    Granola Bars*
  Crispy Rice*
  Puffed Wheat Candy*
  Puffed Wheat*
  Rice Crispy*
  Simple Chocolate Fudge*
  Sweet Ending Pizza*

* Recipe is included in this book. See Index for page number.

"Wurst" Cheese & Lettuce Wrap, page 68

Bag Lunches

A standard, healthy bag lunch should contain a grain product, some fruit or vegetables, a milk or a dairy product and a meat or meat alternative. Add something extra for energy needs and as a special treat. To save time in the morning, prepare your lunch the night before and chill it in the refrigerator.

There are snacks, cookies, candy and squares recipes in this book that could be included in your lunch bag. Also, check the Sandwiches section, pages 50 and 51, for a variety of sandwich and sandwich filling recipes. Combine these with the Bread choices in the Bag Lunch Suggestions chart on pages 10 and 11 and you will never get bored.

Consider how to keep meat and milk products cold. If you place a carton of frozen juice in the bottom of your lunch bag, it will keep your meat or fish sandwich safe to eat until lunchtime and makes a nice slushy drink. A small freezer pack works well, too, or try the following:

FROZEN BANANA: Peel a banana. Cut in half crosswise. Insert into each cut end a flat wooden popsicle stick about halfway. Place each half in a plastic container or bag. Freeze. Include one in your lunch.

FROZEN GRAPES: Freeze a handful of seedless red or green grapes in a plastic container or bag. Include them in your lunch. They will still be cold when it's lunchtime.

FROZEN ORANGES: Cut an orange into quarters. Put them into a plastic container or bag. Freeze. Include them in your lunch.

Ginger Crinkles

GET READY ✓

dry measures, measuring spoons, liquid measures, large bowl, electric mixer, mixing spoon, small bowl, cookie sheet, oven mitts, wire rack, pancake lifter, waxed paper

1.	Hard margarine, softened	1 cup	250 mL
	Granulated sugar	1½ cups	375 mL
	Large egg	1	1
	Dark corn syrup	2 tbsp.	30 mL
	Molasses	½ cup	125 mL
2.	All-purpose flour	3 cups	750 mL
	Baking soda	2 tsp.	10 mL
	Ground cinnamon	2 tsp.	10 mL
	Ground ginger	1 tsp.	5 mL
	Ground cloves	¼ tsp.	1 mL
	Salt	½ tsp.	2 mL
3.	Granulated sugar, for coating	¼ cup	60 mL

Sure to be one of your favorites.

1. Place the oven rack in the center position. Turn the oven on to 375°F (190°C). Measure the first 5 ingredients into the large bowl. Beat with the electric mixer on low speed until blended. Beat on medium speed until smooth.

2. Add the next 6 ingredients. Stir with the mixing spoon until moistened. Roll into 1½ inch (3.8 cm) balls.

3. Put the second amount of sugar into the small bowl. Roll the balls, 1 at a time, in the sugar until completely coated. Arrange the balls 2 inches (5 cm) apart on the ungreased cookie sheet. Bake in the oven for 12 to 14 minutes. Use the oven mitts to remove the cookie sheet to the wire rack. Let stand for 2 minutes. Use the pancake lifter to remove the cookies to the waxed paper on the counter. Cool completely. Makes about 3½ dozen (42) cookies.

This is a very easy cookie to make because it uses a cake mix.

Easy Raisin Cookies

GET READY ✔
cookie sheet, liquid measures, measuring spoons, dry measures, large bowl, mixing spoon, oven mitts, wire rack, pancake lifter, waxed paper

1.			
Yellow cake mix (2 layer size)	1	1
Large eggs, fork-beaten	2	2
Cooking oil	⅓ cup	75 mL
Water	2 tbsp.	30 mL
Raisins	1 cup	250 mL

1. Place the oven rack in the center position. Turn the oven on to 350°F (175°C). Grease the cookie sheet. Combine all 5 ingredients with the mixing spoon in the bowl until moistened and smooth. Small lumps are fine. Drop by tablespoonfuls onto the cookie sheet. Bake in the oven for 18 minutes until golden brown. Use the oven mitts to remove the cookie sheet to the wire rack. Let stand for 2 minutes. Use the pancake lifter to remove the cookies to the waxed paper on the counter. Cool completely. Makes about 3½ dozen (42) cookies.

Careful or the adults will eat all of these.

Corn Flakes Macaroons

GET READY ✓
waxed paper, cookie sheet, large bowl, electric mixer, dry measures, measuring spoons, rubber spatula; oven mitts, wire rack, pancake lifter

1.	**Egg whites (large), room temperature**	**3**	**3**
2.	**Granulated sugar**	**²⁄₃ cup**	**150 mL**
	Vanilla flavoring	**1 tsp.**	**5 mL**
	Corn flakes cereal	**2 cups**	**500 mL**
	Fancy flake coconut	**1 cup**	**250 mL**

1. Place the oven rack in the center position. Turn the oven on to 325°F (160°C). Lay the waxed paper on the ungreased cookie sheet. Beat the egg whites in the bowl with the electric mixer on high speed until foamy.

2. Gradually add the sugar while beating. Add the vanilla. Beat until shiny and stiff peaks form. Fold in the cereal and coconut using the spatula. Drop by tablespoonfuls onto the cookie sheet. Bake in the oven for 20 minutes until lightly browned and crisp. Use the oven mitts to remove the cookie sheet to the wire rack. Let stand for 2 minutes. Use the pancake lifter to remove the cookies to the waxed paper on the counter. Cool completely. Makes about 2½ dozen (30) cookies.

Butterscotch Pudding Cookies

GET READY ✓
measuring spoons, dry measures, medium bowl, mixing spoon, cookie sheet, table fork, oven mitts, wire rack, pancake lifter, waxed paper

1. | | | |
   |---|---|---|
   | Hard margarine, melted | 2 tbsp. | 30 mL |
   | Large egg, fork-beaten | 1 | 1 |
   | Instant butterscotch pudding powder (4 serving size) | 1 | 1 |
   | Biscuit mix | 1 cup | 250 mL |
   | Milk | 1 tbsp. | 15 mL |

1. Place the oven rack in the center position. Turn the oven on to 350°F (175°C). Combine all 5 ingredients with the mixing spoon in the bowl. Shape the dough into balls, using 1 tbsp. (15 mL) dough for each. Place 3 inches (7 cm) apart on the ungreased cookie sheet. Make a crisscross pattern with the fork on top of each ball while lightly pressing down. Bake in the oven for 8 minutes. Use the oven mitts to remove the cookie sheet to the wire rack. Let stand for 2 minutes. Use the pancake lifter to remove the cookies to the waxed paper on the counter. Cool completely. Makes about 1½ dozen (18) cookies.

Variation: Add ½ cup (125 mL) chopped pecans or walnuts.

A very fast and easy way to make cookies.

Lemonade Cookies

GET READY ✔
cookie sheet, dry measures, medium bowl, mixing spoon, measuring spoons, small bowl, oven mitts, wire rack, pancake lifter, waxed paper, pastry brush

1.	Hard margarine, softened	1 cup	250 mL
	Granulated sugar	1 cup	250 mL
	Large eggs	2	2
	Frozen concentrated lemonade	4 tbsp.	60 mL
2.	All-purpose flour	3 cups	750 mL
	Baking soda	1 tsp.	5 mL
	Salt	½ tsp.	2 mL

1. Place the oven rack in the center position. Turn the oven on to 375°F (190°C). Grease the cookie sheet. Cream the margarine and sugar with the mixing spoon in the medium bowl. Beat in the eggs, 1 at a time. Add 2 tbsp. (30 mL) concentrated lemonade.

2. Stir the flour, baking soda and salt in the small bowl. Add to the egg mixture. Mix well. Drop by tablespoonfuls onto the cookie sheet. Bake in the oven for 10 to 12 minutes until light brown. Use the oven mitts to remove the cookie sheet to the wire rack. Let stand for 2 minutes. Use the pancake lifter to remove the cookies to the waxed paper on the counter. Use the pastry brush to brush the tops of the cookies with the remaining 2 tbsp. (30 mL) concentrated lemonade. Cool completely. Makes about 5 dozen (60) cookies.

Pictured on page 19.

Carrot Cookies

GET READY ✔

cookie sheet, dry measures, large bowl, mixing spoon, liquid measures, measuring spoons, oven mitts, wire rack, pancake lifter, waxed paper

1.			
	Hard margarine, softened	½ cup	125 mL
	Granulated sugar	1 cup	250 mL
	Large egg	1	1
	Cooked mashed carrot (or fresh, grated)	1 cup	250 mL
	Milk	⅓ cup	75 mL
	Vanilla flavoring	1 tsp.	5 mL
2.	All-purpose flour	2 cups	500 mL
	Rolled oats (not instant)	2 cups	500 mL
	Baking powder	2 tsp.	10 mL
	Salt	¼ tsp.	1 mL
	Ground cinnamon	1 tsp.	5 mL
	Raisins	1 cup	250 mL

1. Place the oven rack in the center position. Turn the oven on to 375°F (190°C). Grease the cookie sheet. Cream the margarine and sugar well with the mixing spoon in the bowl. Beat in the egg. Add the carrot, milk and vanilla.

2. Add the remaining 6 ingredients. Mix well. Drop by tablespoonfuls onto the cookie sheet. Bake in the oven for 12 to 15 minutes until lightly browned. Use the oven mitts to remove the cookie sheet to the wire rack. Let stand for 2 minutes. Use the pancake lifter to remove the cookies to the waxed paper on the counter. Cool completely. Makes about 4 dozen (48) cookies.

The Carrot Cookies, shown at the top, use leftover or fresh carrots. The Lemonade Cookies, shown at the bottom, are made using frozen concentrated lemonade.

You will have fun making these Rolled Ginger Cookies. Use different cookie cutters to make an assortment of shapes. This recipe is great for making cookies for any special occasion.

Rolled Ginger Cookies

GET READY ✔
cookie sheet, dry measures, large bowl, mixing spoon, liquid measures, measuring spoons, drinking glass, oven mitts, wire rack, pancake lifter, waxed paper

1.			
	Hard margarine, softened	¼ cup	60 mL
	Granulated sugar	½ cup	125 mL
	Fancy (mild) molasses	½ cup	125 mL
	Water	⅓ cup	75 mL
2.	All-purpose flour	3¼ cups	800 mL
	Baking soda	1 tsp.	5 mL
	Ground ginger	1 tsp.	5 mL
	Ground cinnamon	½ tsp.	2 mL
	Ground cloves	¼ tsp.	1 mL
	Salt	½ tsp.	2 mL

1. Place the oven rack in the center position. Turn the oven on to 350°F (175°C). Grease the cookie sheet. Cream the margarine and sugar with the mixing spoon in the bowl. Add the molasses and water.

2. Mix in the remaining 6 ingredients. Shape the dough into 1½ inch (3.8 cm) balls. Place on the cookie sheet. Flatten each ball with the bottom of the glass to ¼ inch (6 mm) thickness. Or roll out to 1/8 inch (3 mm) thickness. Cut out with cookie cutters. Bake in the oven for 8 to 10 minutes. Use the oven mitts to remove the cookie sheet to the wire rack. Let stand for 2 minutes. Use the pancake lifter to remove the cookies to the waxed paper on the counter. Cool completely. Makes about 3 dozen (36) cookies.

Snap Gingers

GET READY ✔

dry measures, medium bowl, mixing spoon, liquid measures, rubber spatula, measuring spoons, cookie sheet, drinking glass, oven mitts, wire rack, pancake lifter, waxed paper

1.	**Hard margarine, softened**	½ cup	125 mL
	Granulated sugar	⅔ cup	150 mL
2.	**Fancy (mild) molasses**	¼ cup	60 mL
	Large egg, fork-beaten	1	1
3.	**All-purpose flour**	1½ cups	375 mL
	Baking soda	1½ tsp.	7 mL
	Ground ginger	1½ tsp.	7 mL
	Salt	¼ tsp.	1 mL
4.	**Granulated sugar, for coating**		

1. Place the oven rack in the center position. Turn the oven on to 375°F (190°C). Cream the margarine and first amount of sugar well with the mixing spoon in the bowl.

2. Stir in the molasses and egg until well mixed, occasionally scraping down the sides of the bowl with the rubber spatula.

3. Stir in the next 4 ingredients until well blended.

4. Shape the dough into 1 inch (2.5 cm) balls. Roll each ball in the second amount of sugar until well coated. Place the balls 2 inches (5 cm) apart on the ungreased cookie sheet. Flatten each ball with the bottom of the glass to ¼ inch (6 mm) thickness. Bake in the oven for 7 minutes. Use the oven mitts to remove the cookie sheet to the wire rack. Let stand for 1 minute. Use the pancake lifter to remove the cookies to the waxed paper. Cool completely. Makes about 2 dozen (24) cookies.

A chewy cookie with ginger flavor through and through.

Stick Dip

GET READY ✔

measuring spoons, small bowl, mixing spoon

1. **Sour cream**   3 tbsp.   50 mL
    Beef bouillon powder   ½ tsp.   2 mL
    Onion salt   ¼ tsp.   1 mL

1. Combine all 3 ingredients with the mixing spoon in the bowl. Makes 3 tbsp. (50 mL) dip.

    Pictured on page 13.

Garlic Mustard Dip

GET READY ✔

dry measures, measuring spoons, small bowl, mixing spoon, plastic wrap

1. **Salad dressing (or mayonnaise)**   ⅓ cup   75 mL
    Sour cream   ⅔ cup   150 mL
    Prepared mustard   1 tbsp.   15 mL
    Garlic powder   ⅛ tsp.   0.5 mL
    Salt, sprinkle
    Pepper, sprinkle

1. Combine all 6 ingredients with the mixing spoon in the bowl. Cover with plastic wrap. Chill for 30 minutes to blend the flavors. Makes 1¼ cups (300 mL) dip.

Garlic Mustard Dip
is great with fresh
veggies.

Honey Mustard Dunk

GET READY ✔

dry measures, measuring spoons, small bowl, mixing spoon

1.	Salad dressing (or mayonnaise)	½ cup	125 mL
	Liquid honey	2 tbsp.	30 mL
	Prepared mustard	2 tsp.	10 mL

1. Combine all 3 ingredients with the mixing spoon in the bowl until smooth. Makes ⅔ cup (150 mL) dip.

> The next time you have fresh veggies for a snack, try Garlic Mustard Dip, shown at the top, or Caesar Dip, shown at the bottom.

Caesar Dip

GET READY ✔

dry measures, measuring spoons, small bowl, mixing spoon

1.	Salad dressing (or mayonnaise)	½ cup	125 mL
	Sour cream	½ cup	125 mL
	Lemon juice	1 tbsp.	15 mL
	Garlic clove, crushed (or ¼ tsp., 1 mL, powder)	1	1
	Salt	⅛ tsp.	0.5 mL
	Pepper	⅛ tsp.	0.5 mL
	Prepared mustard	1 tsp.	5 mL
	Grated Parmesan cheese	1 tbsp.	15 mL
	Parsley flakes	1 tsp.	5 mL

1. Combine all 9 ingredients with the mixing spoon in the bowl until smooth. Let stand for 15 minutes to blend the flavors. Makes ¾ cup (175 mL) dip.

Pepper-Corn Crackers

GET READY ✔
dry measures, measuring spoons, medium bowl, mixing spoon, pastry blender, cookie sheet, table fork, oven mitts, wire rack

1.	All-purpose flour	¾ cup	175 mL
	Corn flakes cereal	3 cups	750 mL
	Baking powder	¼ tsp.	1 mL
	Grated Cheddar (or Gouda or Edam or Monterey Jack) cheese	2 cups	500 mL
2.	Hard margarine	½ cup	125 mL
3.	Finely diced red pepper	½ cup	125 mL
4.	Paprika, sprinkle		

A soft and chewy cracker. A perfect addition to your lunch. These freeze well.

1. Place the oven rack in the center position. Turn the oven on to 350°F (175°C). Combine the flour, cereal and baking powder with the mixing spoon in the bowl. Add the cheese. Stir well.

2. Cut in the margarine with the pastry blender until the mixture looks crumbly, with pieces no bigger than the size of a small pea. The mixture should almost want to stick together.

3. Work with your hands until a stiff dough forms. Work in the red pepper.

4. Shape the dough into 1 inch (2.5 cm) balls. Place the balls on the ungreased cookie sheet. Make a crisscross pattern with the fork on top of each ball while lightly pressing down. Sprinkle with the paprika. Bake in the oven for 15 minutes until golden brown. Use the oven mitts to remove the baking sheet to the wire rack. Cool completely. Makes 40 crackers.

Crispy Chicken Cracky

GET READY ✔
baking sheet, sharp knife, cutting board, medium bowl, dry measures, microwave-safe bowl, measuring spoons, mixing spoon, plastic freezer bag, oven mitts, wire rack

1.	Boneless, skinless chicken breast halves (about 1 lb., 454 g)	4	4
2.	Margarine	¼ cup	60 mL
	Worcestershire sauce (optional)	1 tsp.	5 mL
	Salt	½ tsp.	2 mL
	Pepper	¼ tsp.	1 mL
3.	Soda cracker crumbs (see Note)	⅔ cup	150 mL

1. Place the oven rack in the center position. Turn the oven on to 400°F (205°C). Lightly grease the baking sheet. Cut each chicken breast with the knife into 6 chunks on the cutting board. Place in the medium bowl.

2. Microwave the margarine in the microwave-safe bowl on high (100%) for about 30 seconds until melted. Add the Worcestershire sauce, salt and pepper. Stir with the mixing spoon. Drizzle the margarine mixture over the chicken. Stir until well coated.

3. Put the cracker crumbs into the bag. Put 3 or 4 pieces of chicken at a time into the crumbs, shaking until well coated. Place the coated chicken on the baking sheet. Bake in the oven for 18 to 20 minutes until crisp and golden brown. Use the oven mitts to remove the baking sheet to the wire rack. Cool. Makes 24 chunks.

Eat hot or cold with Garlic Mustard Dip, page 22, or Honey Mustard Dunk, page 23.

Note: To make crumbs, place the crackers in a plastic freezer bag. Roll with a rolling pin.

Ham & Melon Kabobs

GET READY ✓

six 4 inch (10 cm) wooden bamboo skewers (or cocktail picks)

1. | Cantaloupe cubes (¾ inch, 2 cm, size) | 12 | 12 |
    | Ham cubes (¾ inch, 2 cm, size) | 6 | 6 |

1. Push 1 cube of the cantaloupe, 1 cube of the ham, and another cube of cantaloupe on each skewer. Makes 6 kabobs.

Variation: 6 pieces of shaved ham, rolled or folded into 1 inch (2.5 cm) pieces, may be substituted for the ham cubes.

Pack in a covered container to take to school.

This is perfect for sandwich meat. Slices well when cold. Freeze individual slices for your lunch.

Quick Turkey Loaf

GET READY ✓
9 × 5 × 3 inch (22 × 12.5 × 7.5 cm) loaf pan, dry measures, measuring spoons, blender, large bowl, mixing spoon, oven mitts, wire rack

1.			
	Large egg	1	1
	Ketchup	⅓ cup	75 mL
	Seasoning salt	1½ tsp.	7 mL
	Pepper	⅛ tsp.	0.5 mL
	Small onion, cut into chunks	1	1
	Large carrot, cut into chunks	1	1
	Large celery rib, cut into chunks	1	1
2.	Lean ground turkey (or chicken)	1½ lbs.	680 g
	Large flake rolled oats (old-fashioned)	⅔ cup	150 mL

1. Place the oven rack in the center position. Turn the oven on to 350°F (175°C). Grease the loaf pan. Combine the egg, ketchup, seasoning salt and pepper in the blender. Place the lid on the blender. Process until smooth. While the blender is processing, gradually add the onion, carrot and celery, a few pieces at a time, through the opening in the lid. Process until almost smooth. There will be some very small chunks of vegetable remaining.

2. Put the ground turkey into the bowl. Add the vegetable mixture. Stir well with the mixing spoon. Stir in the rolled oats. Let stand for 10 minutes. Pack into the loaf pan. Bake in the oven for 1¼ hours. Use the oven mitts to remove the pan to the wire rack. Let stand for 5 minutes. Cuts into 10 slices.

Macaroni & Cottage Cheese

GET READY ✔

liquid measures, measuring spoons, medium saucepan, dry measures, long-handled mixing spoon, colander, frying pan

1.	Water	4 cups	1 L
	Salt	1 tsp.	5 mL
	Elbow macaroni (or small shell pasta), uncooked	1½ cups	375 mL
2.	Margarine	2 tsp.	10 mL
	Finely chopped onion	⅓ cup	75 mL
	Imitation bacon bits (or 1 bacon slice, cooked crisp and crumbled)	1 tbsp.	15 mL
	Creamed cottage cheese	1¼ cups	300 mL
	Salt, sprinkle		
	Pepper, sprinkle		

A new twist to an old favorite.

1. Bring the water and first amount of salt to a boil in the saucepan. Add the macaroni. Boil, uncovered, for 7 to 9 minutes, stirring occasionally, just until tender. Drain the pasta in the colander. Rinse with hot water. Drain. Return the pasta to the saucepan. Cover to keep warm.

2. Melt the margarine in the frying pan. Add the onion. Sauté using the mixing spoon until soft and golden brown. Add the bacon bits. Add the onion mixture to the pasta. Stir in the cottage cheese. Sprinkle with the second amount of salt and pepper. Cool. Reheat in the microwave at school. Makes 4 cups (1 L) mac and cheese.

Pickles add a delicious crunch. Eat now or cover and chill overnight for tomorrow's lunch.

Pickly Pita Pockets

GET READY ✔

dry measures, measuring spoons, small bowl, mixing spoon

1.	Diced ham (or beef roast or salami)	1 cup	250 mL
	Finely chopped dill pickle, blotted dry with paper towel	⅓ cup	75 mL
	Salad dressing (or mayonnaise)	2 tbsp.	30 mL
	Prepared mustard	1 tsp.	5 mL
2.	Pita breads (6 inch, 15 cm, size), cut in half	2	2

1. Combine the ham, pickle, salad dressing and mustard with the mixing spoon in the bowl.

2. Fill each pita half with ⅓ cup (75 mL) filling. Makes 4 pita halves.

Cake mix makes a very easy start to these muffins.

Lemon Blueberry Muffins

GET READY ✔
18 muffin papers, 2 muffin pans (for 18 muffins), dry measures, large bowl, mixing spoon, rubber spatula, wooden toothpick, oven mitts, wire rack

1.	Lemon cake mix (2 layer size)	1	1
	Large eggs, fork-beaten	2	2
	Sour cream	1½ cups	375 mL
2.	Frozen blueberries	2 cups	500 mL

1. Place the oven rack in the center position. Turn the oven on to 325°F (160°C). Place the muffin papers in the pans. Combine the cake mix, eggs and sour cream in the bowl. Stir with the mixing spoon until well blended. The batter will be stiff.

2. Lightly fold in the blueberries with the spatula. Divide the batter among the 18 muffin cups. Bake in the oven for 40 minutes until golden brown. The toothpick inserted in the center of 2 or 3 muffins should come out clean. Use the oven mitts to remove the muffin pans to the wire rack. Let stand for 10 minutes. Remove the muffins to the rack to cool completely. Makes 18 muffins.

Date & Nut Muffins

GET READY ✔

muffin pan (for 12 muffins), dry measures, measuring spoons, large bowl, mixing spoon, liquid measures, blender, wooden toothpick, oven mitts, wire rack

1.			
	All-purpose flour	1½ cups	375 mL
	Whole wheat flour	½ cup	125 mL
	Baking powder	1 tbsp.	15 mL
	Brown sugar, packed	¼ cup	60 mL
	Chopped walnuts	½ cup	125 mL
2.	Milk	1 cup	250 mL
	Large egg	1	1
	Cooking oil	¼ cup	60 mL
	Maple flavoring	½ tsp.	2 mL
	Chopped dates	½ cup	125 mL

1. Place the oven rack in the center position. Turn the oven on to 375°F (190°C). Grease the muffin pan. Combine the first 5 ingredients with the mixing spoon in the bowl. Make a well in the center.

2. Measure the remaining 5 ingredients into the blender. Place the lid on the blender. Process for 5 to 10 seconds. Pour the wet ingredients into the well in the flour mixture. Stir just to moisten. Divide the batter among the 12 muffin cups. Bake in the oven for 20 minutes until golden brown. The toothpick inserted in the center of 2 or 3 muffins should come out clean. Use the oven mitts to remove the muffin pan to the wire rack. Let stand for 10 minutes. Remove the muffins to the rack to cool completely. Makes 12 muffins.

A great snack for any time of the day.

Orange Cranberry Muffins

1.			
Medium navel orange, washed	1	1
Prepared orange juice	½ cup	125 mL
Large egg	1	1
Hard margarine	½ cup	125 mL
Dried cranberries	½ cup	125 mL

2.			
All-purpose flour	1¾ cups	425 mL
Baking powder	1 tsp.	5 mL
Baking soda	1 tsp.	5 mL
Granulated sugar	⅔ cup	150 mL
Salt	½ tsp.	2 mL

Using the entire orange gives these muffins lots of vitamins and minerals.

1. Place the oven rack in the center position. Turn the oven on to 400°F (205°C). Grease the muffin pan. Cut the orange with the knife into 8 pieces on the cutting board. Put into the blender. Add the orange juice. Place the lid on the blender. Process for 1½ minutes until the orange peel is finely chopped. Add the egg and margarine. Process until blended. Add the dried cranberries. Process for 2 seconds.

2. Combine the remaining 5 ingredients with the mixing spoon in the large bowl. Make a well in the center. Pour the wet ingredients into the well. Stir just to moisten. Divide the batter among the 12 muffin cups. Bake in the oven for 15 minutes until golden brown. The toothpick inserted in the center of 2 or 3 muffins should come out clean. Use the oven mitts to remove the muffin pan to the wire rack. Let stand for 10 minutes. Remove the muffins to the rack to cool completely. Makes 12 muffins.

Moist and delicious.

Apple Granola Muffins

GET READY ✔
muffin pan (for 12 muffins), dry measures, measuring spoons, medium bowl, mixing spoon, pastry blender, liquid measures, wooden toothpick, oven mitts, wire rack

1.			
	All-purpose flour	2 cups	500 mL
	Baking powder	4 tsp.	20 mL
	Salt	1 tsp.	5 mL
	Brown sugar, packed	3 tbsp.	50 mL
	Ground cinnamon	½ tsp.	2 mL
2.	Hard margarine	⅓ cup	75 mL
	Medium apple, cored and chopped	1	1
	Milk	1 cup	250 mL
	Vanilla flavoring	1 tsp.	5 mL
3.	Granola cereal	¼ cup	60 mL

1. Place the oven rack in the center position. Turn the oven on to 400°F (205°C). Grease the muffin pan. Combine the first 5 ingredients with the mixing spoon in the bowl.

2. Cut the margarine in with the pastry blender until the mixture looks crumbly. Add the apple, milk and vanilla. Stir just to moisten. Divide the batter among the 12 muffin cups.

3. Sprinkle each with 1 tsp. (5 mL) cereal. Bake in the oven for 20 minutes until golden brown. The toothpick inserted in the center of 2 or 3 muffins should come out clean. Use the oven mitts to remove the muffin pan to the wire rack. Let stand for 10 minutes. Remove the muffins to the rack to cool completely. Makes 12 muffins.

So colorful, juicy and tasty. Choose from a variety of fresh fruits. Do not freeze.

Fruit Salad

 GET READY ✓

covered container, mixing spoon

1.			
Watermelon chunks		6	6
Kiwifruit slices, cut in half		3	3
Cantaloupe chunks		4	4
Orange segments, cut in half		3	3
Seedless red or green grapes (or both)		6	6
Apple (or pear) slices (or both), dipped into fruit (or lemon) juice to keep from browning		3	3

1. Combine all 6 ingredients in the container. Stir with the mixing spoon. Place the lid on the container. Makes about 2 cups (500 mL) salad.

Salad Lunch

GET READY ✔

medium covered container, small covered container

1.	Chopped iceberg lettuce	½ cup	125 mL
	Tomato wedges	2	2
	Cucumber slices	3	3
	Celery stick	1	1
	1 inch (2.5 cm) cubes of Cheddar cheese	2	2
	Thin carrot sticks	3	3
	Large hard-boiled egg	½	½

2. **Stick Dip, page 22**

1. Put the first 7 ingredients into the medium container. Place the lid on the container.
2. Put the dip into the small container. Place the lid on the container. Serves 1.

Cottage Cheese Salad

GET READY ✔

dry measures, measuring spoons, small bowl, mixing spoon

1.	Creamed cottage cheese	1 cup	250 mL
	Diced cucumber, with peel	¼ cup	60 mL
	Grated carrot	2 tbsp.	30 mL
	Diced red pepper	2 tbsp.	30 mL
	Garlic salt	⅛ tsp.	0.5 mL
	Pepper, sprinkle		
	Celery seed, sprinkle		

1. Combine all 7 ingredients with the mixing spoon in the bowl. Let stand for 10 minutes to blend the flavors. Chill for up to 24 hours. Makes 1½ cups (375 mL) salad.

Very colorful. A great blend of flavors.

A colorful and tasty salad.

Tortellini Salad

GET READY ✓
liquid measures, measuring spoons, small saucepan, dry measures, colander,
medium bowl, mixing spoon, plastic wrap

1.	Water	6 cups	1.5 L
	Salt	1 tsp.	5 mL
	Fresh (or dried) cheese-filled tortellini	1 cup	250 mL
2.	Diced cucumber, with peel	½ cup	125 mL
	Small tomato, diced	1	1
	Thinly sliced green onion	¼ cup	60 mL
	Thinly slivered green or red pepper	½ cup	125 mL
	Salt	½ tsp.	2 mL
	Pepper	⅛ tsp.	0.5 mL

1. Bring the water and salt to a boil in the saucepan. Add the tortellini. Heat for about 10 minutes until tender but still firm. Drain in the colander. Rinse with cold water until cool. Drain well.

2. Combine the pasta and the remaining 6 ingredients with the mixing spoon in the bowl. Cover with plastic wrap. Chill for 30 minutes to blend the flavors. Makes 3½ cups (875 mL) salad.

Bean & Tomato Salad

GET READY ✔
dry measures, medium bowl, mixing spoon, measuring spoons, small bowl, plastic wrap

1. Can of garbanzo beans (chick peas), drained and rinsed	19 oz.	540 mL
Thinly sliced celery	½ cup	125 mL
Green onion, thinly sliced	1	1
Diced red pepper	½ cup	125 mL
Can of stewed tomatoes, drained and chopped	14 oz.	398 mL
2. DRESSING		
Olive (or cooking) oil	2 tbsp.	30 mL
White vinegar	2 tbsp.	30 mL
Dried sweet basil	½ tsp.	2 mL
Dry mustard	¼ tsp.	1 mL
Garlic powder	⅛ tsp.	0.5 mL
Parsley flakes	2 tsp.	10 mL

1. Combine the first 5 ingredients with the mixing spoon in the medium bowl.

2. **Dressing:** Combine the remaining 6 ingredients in the small bowl. Pour over the vegetable mixture. Mix well. Cover with plastic wrap. Chill for several hours or overnight, stirring several times. Chill for up to 3 days. Makes 4 cups (1 L) salad.

A delicious, crunchy salad. Perfect to take to school for lunch.

Crunchy Potato Salad

GET READY ✔
sharp knife, cutting board, liquid measures, measuring spoons, small saucepan, colander, medium bowl, mixing spoon, plastic wrap

1.	Large potato	1	1
	Water	1 cup	250 mL
	Salt	¼ tsp.	1 mL
2.	Diced red pepper	2 tbsp.	30 mL
	Grated carrot	1 tbsp.	15 mL
	Finely diced celery	1 tbsp.	15 mL
	Sliced green onion	1 tbsp.	15 mL
	Grated Cheddar cheese	2 tbsp.	30 mL
	Italian dressing	2 tbsp.	30 mL
	Salt, sprinkle		
	Pepper, sprinkle		

1. Cut the potato crosswise with the knife into 3 pieces on the cutting board. Put the potato pieces, water and salt into the saucepan. Bring to a boil on high. Reduce the heat to low. Cover. Simmer for about 13 minutes until the potato is tender when poked with the knife. Do not overcook or the potato will be mushy. Drain in the colander. Cool slightly. Dice into small cubes on the cutting board.

2. Combine the potato and the remaining 8 ingredients with the mixing spoon in the bowl. Cover with plastic wrap. Chill until cold. Makes 1½ cups (375 mL) salad.

Very colorful. Watch the cooking time of the potato. It will differ according to the size of your potato.

Make this salad the night before to take to school the next day. A crunchy, refreshing salad.

Cucumber & Pea Salad

GET READY ✔

dry measures, measuring spoons, small bowl, mixing spoon, small cup

1.	Diced cucumber, with peel	1 cup	250 mL
	Frozen baby peas, thawed	½ cup	125 mL
	Sliced green onion	2 tbsp.	30 mL
	Garlic salt, sprinkle		
	Pepper, sprinkle		
	Cubed Cheddar (or Swiss) cheese	½ cup	125 mL
	(½ inch, 12 mm, size)		
2.	**DRESSING**		
	Salad dressing (or mayonnaise)	2 tbsp.	30 mL
	Granulated sugar	2 tsp.	10 mL
	Lemon juice	1 tsp.	5 mL

1. Combine the first 6 ingredients with the mixing spoon in the bowl.

2. **Dressing:** Mix the salad dressing, sugar and lemon juice in the cup. Add to the vegetable mixture. Mix well. Makes 2 cups (500 mL) salad.

This salad can also be stuffed into a pita bread for a salad sandwich.

Rice Salad

GET READY ✓

dry measures, measuring spoons, small bowl, mixing spoon

1.			
Cooked rice (your favorite)	¾ cup	175 mL
Cooked ham, chopped	2 oz.	57 g
Sliced green onion	2 tbsp.	30 mL
Cooked vegetables (such as peas, broccoli florets or green beans)	½ cup	125 mL
Grated carrot	¼ cup	60 mL
Olive (or cooking) oil	1 tsp.	5 mL
White (or red wine or apple cider) vinegar	2 tsp.	10 mL
Salt, sprinkle		

1. Combine all 8 ingredients with the mixing spoon in the bowl. Makes 1½ cups (375 mL) salad.

Variation: Add 2 tbsp. (30 mL) sunflower seeds or pumpkin seeds, or add ¼ cup (60 mL) raisins.

Tomato & Mozza Salad

GET READY ✔
sharp knife, cutting board, paper towel, small bowl, measuring spoons, mixing spoon, dry measures

1.	Medium tomatoes	2	2
2.	Olive (or cooking) oil	2 tsp.	10 mL
	Garlic salt	¼ tsp.	1 mL
	Pepper, sprinkle		
	Dried sweet basil	¼ tsp.	1 mL
	Sliced green onion	1 tbsp.	15 mL
	Ripe olives, sliced (optional)	4	4
3.	Grated mozzarella cheese	½ cup	125 mL

1. Cut the tomatoes in half with the knife on the cutting board. Gently squeeze the tomato halves over the paper towel to remove the seeds. Discard the seeds and juice. Dice the tomato into bite-size pieces. Place in the bowl.

2. Add the next 6 ingredients. Stir with the mixing spoon.

3. Stir in the cheese. Makes 1½ cups (375 mL) salad.

Variation: Spoon salad onto baguette slices. Place the slices on a baking sheet. Broil on the top rack in the oven until the cheese is melted.

This salad tastes even better when left to stand awhile. Great to take for lunch.

Pronounced muhf-ful-LEHT-tuh. Make this New Orleans sandwich the night before to take for lunch the next day.

Muffuletta

GET READY ✓

measuring spoons, small cup, pastry brush, dry measures

1.			
Italian-style crusty bun, cut in half horizontally	1	1
Italian dressing	1½ tbsp.	25 mL
Tomato slices	4	4
Mozzarella cheese slices	2	2
Lean ham (or beef) slices (about 2 oz., 57 g)	2	2
Alfalfa sprouts (or shredded lettuce)	⅓ cup	75 mL

1. Pull out bits of bread from the soft center of both bun halves, making a shallow hollow. Put the dressing into the cup. Use the pastry brush to spread about ½ tbsp. (7 mL) dressing on each bun half. Layer 2 slices of tomato, 1 slice of cheese and 1 slice of ham on the bottom half of the bun. Brush the remaining dressing on the ham. Top with the sprouts, remaining cheese slice, remaining tomato slices and remaining ham slice. Cover with the top half of the bun. Makes 1 sandwich.

Tuna Biscuits

GET READY ✔
muffin pan (for 8 large or 16 mini muffins), dry measures, measuring spoons, medium bowl, whisk, mixing spoon, oven mitts, wire rack

1.	Large eggs, fork-beaten	2	2
	Salad dressing (or mayonnaise)	¼ cup	60 mL
	Margarine, melted	2 tbsp.	30 mL
	Lemon juice	½ tbsp.	7 mL
	Hot pepper sauce	⅛ tsp.	0.5 mL
2.	Cheese-flavored crackers, coarsely crushed	22	22
	Can of white tuna, packed in water, drained and broken into chunks	6½ oz.	184 g
	Green onion, sliced	1	1
	Finely diced green pepper (optional)	2 tbsp.	30 mL

1. Place the oven rack in the center position. Turn the oven on to 375°F (190°C). Grease 8 large cups, or 16 mini cups, in the muffin pan. Combine the egg, salad dressing, margarine, lemon juice and hot pepper sauce in the bowl. Beat with the whisk until well blended.

2. Stir the cracker crumbs into the egg mixture with the mixing spoon. Add the tuna, green onion and green pepper. Stir well. Fill the muffin cups ¾ full with the batter. Bake in the oven for 20 minutes for the large cups or for 15 minutes for the mini cups. Use the oven mitts to remove the pan to the wire rack. Makes 8 large biscuits or 16 mini biscuits.

Very tasty. Great to take for lunch instead of a sandwich.

Yummy to eat for lunch any day of the week.

Ham & Cuke Sandwich

 GET READY ✔
measuring spoons, small bowl, mixing spoon, table knife, bread knife, cutting board

1.	Salad dressing (or mayonnaise)	2 tsp.	10 mL
	French (or Russian) dressing	2 tsp.	10 mL
	Whole wheat (or white) bread slices	2	2
2.	Shaved ham slices (about 2 oz., 57 g)	2	2
	Cucumber slices, with peel	3-4	3-4

1. Combine the salad dressing and French dressing with the mixing spoon in the bowl. Spread the mixture on both slices of bread with the table knife.

2. Place the ham slices on 1 slice of bread. Top with the cucumber slices. Cover with the second slice of bread. Cut in half with the bread knife on the cutting board. Makes 1 sandwich.

Tuna Buns

GET READY ✓

measuring spoons, dry measures, medium bowl, mixing spoon, frying pan, pancake lifter, table knife

1.	Can of tuna in water, with liquid, flaked	6½ oz.	184 g
	Large egg, fork-beaten	1	1
	Minced onion flakes	1 tsp.	5 mL
	Small carrot, grated	1	1
	Fine dry bread crumbs	½ cup	125 mL
	Parsley flakes	1 tsp.	5 mL
	Lemon juice	1 tsp.	5 mL
	Salt, sprinkle		
	Pepper, sprinkle		
2.	Cooking oil	1 tsp.	5 mL
3.	Salad dressing (or mayonnaise)	2 tbsp.	30 mL
	Kaiser rolls, cut in half horizontally	4	4
	Lettuce leaves	4	4

1. Combine the first 9 ingredients with the mixing spoon in the bowl. Form into 4 patties.

2. Heat the cooking oil in the frying pan on medium. Put the patties into the frying pan. Cook the patties for about 2 minutes until golden brown. Turn the patties over with the pancake lifter. Cook for 2 minutes until golden brown and crispy.

3. Spread the salad dressing with the knife on the bottom half of each roll. Place 1 patty on top of the salad dressing. Top with the lettuce. Cover with the top halves of the rolls. Makes 4 buns.

Great warm or cold.

Pepper Cheese Roll

GET READY ✔

bread knife, cutting board, measuring spoons, pastry brush, dry measures

1.	Whole wheat roll, oblong (or oval) shaped (about 5 inches, 12.5 cm, long)	1	1
	Italian dressing	1 tbsp.	15 mL
2.	Red, orange or yellow pepper, cut into thin strips	½	½
	Pepper, sprinkle		
	Dried sweet basil, just a pinch		
	White cheese (such as mozzarella, Swiss or Monterey Jack), thinly sliced	2 oz.	57 g
	Alfalfa (or mixed) sprouts (optional)	¼ cup	60 mL

1. Cut the roll in half horizontally with the bread knife on the cutting board. Pull out bits of bread from the soft center of both roll halves, making a shallow hollow. Use the pastry brush to spread about ½ tbsp. (7 mL) dressing on each roll half.

2. Lay the pepper strips lengthwise on the bottom half. Sprinkle with the pepper and basil. Lay the cheese slices on the pepper strips. Spread the sprouts on the cheese. Cover with the top half of the roll. Makes 1 sandwich.

This can be made ahead, wrapped with plastic wrap and chilled for up to two days.

These will freeze well. Simply thaw before heating, or pop in your lunch bag in the morning and by noon the sub is well thawed. A great lunch!

Super Sausage Sub

GET READY ✔
non-stick frying pan, long-handled mixing spoon, colander, measuring spoons, liquid measures, dry measures

1.			
Ground sausage meat	1 lb.	454 g
Medium green pepper, cut into slivers	1	1
Medium onion, sliced	1	1
Pepper	⅛ tsp.	0.5 mL
Paprika	½ tsp.	2 mL
Cayenne pepper, sprinkle		
Meatless spaghetti sauce	1 cup	250 mL
2.			
Submarine buns (10 inches, 25 cm, long), cut in half horizontally	4	4
Grated Cheddar (or mozzarella) cheese	1 cup	250 mL

1. Scramble-fry the sausage in the frying pan on medium for 10 minutes using the mixing spoon, breaking up any large lumps. Drain in the colander. Add the green pepper, onion, pepper, paprika and cayenne pepper. Scramble-fry for 10 minutes until the vegetables are tender-crisp and the sausage is no longer pink. Stir in the spaghetti sauce. Remove from the heat. Makes 3 cups (750 mL) sauce.

2. Pull out bits of bread from the soft center of both bun halves, making a shallow hollow. Divide the sausage mixture among the 4 bottom halves of the buns. Top each with ¼ cup (60 mL) cheese. Cover with the top halves of the buns. Makes 4 sandwiches.

Variation: These can be heated in the microwave oven on medium (50%) for 1 minute or wrapped with foil and heated in a 300°F (150°C) oven for 15 minutes.

Hero Sandwich

GET READY ✔

bread knife, cutting board, measuring spoons, table knife

1.	Submarine bun (12 inches, 30 cm, long)	1	1
	Salad dressing (or mayonnaise)	1 tbsp.	15 mL
	Prepared mustard	2 tsp.	10 mL
2.	Thin slices of salami (about 1½ oz., 42 g)	6	6
	Thinly shaved deli ham (or chicken or turkey)	1½ oz.	42 g
	Tomato slices	5	5
	Mozzarella (or Monterey Jack) cheese, thinly sliced	2 oz.	57 g
	Shredded lettuce (or mixed sprouts)	½ cup	125 mL
	Salt, sprinkle		
	Pepper, sprinkle		

1. Cut the submarine bun in half horizontally on the cutting board with the bread knife. Pull out bits of bread from the soft center of both bun halves, making a shallow hollow. Spread the salad dressing on each half with the table knife. Spread the mustard on the salad dressing.

2. Layer the next 5 ingredients on top of the mustard on bottom bun half in the order given. Sprinkle with the salt and pepper. Cover with the top half of the bun. Cut in half on the cutting board with the bread knife. Makes 1 sandwich.

You will be a hero if you can finish this! You will be an even bigger hero if you share!

Peanut Butter & Pickle Sandwich

GET READY ✔

measuring spoons, table knife, paper towel, bread knife, cutting board

1.	**Peanut butter**	**2 tbsp.**	**30 mL**
	White (or whole wheat) bread slices	**2**	**2**
2.	**Dill pickle(s), cut in half lengthwise**	**1-2**	**1-2**

1. Spread the peanut butter with the table knife on 1 side of each bread slice.

2. Lay the pickle halves on the paper towel for 1 to 2 minutes to soak up the juice. Lay both halves on top of the peanut butter. Cover with the second slice of bread, peanut butter side down. Cut in half with the bread knife on the cutting board. Makes 1 sandwich.

Variation: Spread peanut butter on a flour tortilla. Lay a small whole dill pickle on top of the tortilla at 1 end. Roll the tortilla around the pickle.

Who would have thought! Sounds interesting—and very tasty!

Sandwiches

Baked Bean Sandwich: Spread drained beans (or drained and mashed), on 1 slice of buttered bread. Add some chopped cooked sausage, ground meat or wieners. Cover with the second slice of buttered bread.

Beef Sandwich: Spread mustard, ketchup or salad dressing (or mayonnaise) on 1 slice of buttered bread. Add slices of cold roast beef. Top with lettuce or alfalfa sprouts. The lettuce will stay crisper if on the side not touching the salad dressing. Cover with the second slice of buttered bread.

Cheese & Lettuce Sandwich: Spread salad dressing (or mayonnaise) or sandwich spread on 1 slice of buttered bread. Lay a cheese slice on the salad dressing. Top with lettuce. The lettuce will stay crisper if on the side not touching the salad dressing. Cover with the second slice of buttered bread.

Cheese & Tomato Sandwich: Spread salad dressing (or mayonnaise) or sandwich spread on 1 slice of buttered bread. Lay a cheese slice on top. Cover the cheese with tomato slices. Sprinkle with salt and pepper. Cover with the second slice of buttered bread.

Cheese Sandwich: Lay a slice of Swiss or Cheddar cheese on 1 slice of buttered bread. Or spread with processed cheese spread. Cover with the second slice of buttered bread.

Chicken Sandwich or Roll: Butter 2 slices of bread or the inside surfaces of a roll. Using leftover cooked chicken, slice enough to cover 1 bread slice. Either a bit of cranberry sauce or some leftover stuffing is a tasty addition. Cover with the second slice of buttered bread.

Ham & Cheese Sandwich: Spread mustard, salad dressing (or mayonnaise) or sandwich spread on 1 slice of buttered bread. Add a slice of ham and a slice of cheese. Cover with the second slice of buttered bread.

Ham & Lettuce Sandwich: Spread mustard or salad dressing (or mayonnaise) on 1 slice of buttered bread. Put a slice of ham on top. Add some lettuce. The lettuce will stay crisper if on the side not touching the salad dressing. Cover with the second slice of buttered bread.

Ham & Tomato Sandwich: Spread mustard, salad dressing (or mayonnaise) or sandwich spread on 1 slice of buttered bread. Add a slice of ham and a slice of tomato. Cover with the second slice of buttered bread.

Hamburger: Lay a cooked meat patty on the bottom half of a buttered hamburger bun. Spread ketchup, mustard and relish on the top half of the bun. You can also add onions (raw or cooked), pickles, cheese slice or tomatoes.

Hot Dog: Lay a hot wiener on the bottom half of a buttered hot dog bun. Spread ketchup, relish and mustard on the top half. You can also add onions (raw or cooked), cheese (slice or grated), and a cooked strip of bacon. A delicious hot dog has a narrow slice of cheese and a slice of cooked bacon alongside of the wiener.

PBBS: Do try a Peanut Butter Banana Sandwich. Spread peanut butter on 1 slice of buttered bread. Place a layer of banana slices on top. Cover with the second slice of buttered bread.

Peanut Butter Sandwich: Spread peanut butter on 1 slice of buttered bread. Cover with the second slice of buttered bread.

Submarine: Split and butter a submarine bun. Layer the bottom half with cheese slices, cold meat slices, tomato slices and lettuce. Spread salad dressing (or mayonnaise) and mustard on the top half of the bun. Cover with the top half of the bun.

Cool completely. Store any extra mixture in a covered container.

Spiced Nuts

GET READY ✔
measuring spoons, 10 inch (25 cm) glass pie plate (or small microwave-safe casserole dish), mixing spoon, dry measures, oven mitts, hot pad, paper towel, large plate

1.	Margarine	2 tbsp.	30 mL
2.	Soy sauce	1 tsp.	5 mL
	Lemon juice	1 tsp.	5 mL
	Ground ginger	¼ tsp.	1 mL
	Garlic powder	⅛ tsp.	0.5 mL
	Onion powder	⅛ tsp.	0.5 mL
	Salt	¼ tsp.	1 mL
3.	Walnut (or pecan) halves	¾ cup	175 mL
	Whole blanched almonds	¾ cup	175 mL

1. Measure the margarine into the pie plate. Microwave on high (100%) for 20 to 30 seconds until melted.

2. Add the next 6 ingredients. Stir well with the mixing spoon.

3. Add the walnuts and almonds. Stir. Microwave on high (100%) for 2 minutes. Stir. Repeat in 2 minute intervals until the nuts are toasted. This will take about 10 minutes. Use the oven mitts to remove the pie plate to the hot pad. Lay the paper towel on the large plate. Use the oven mitts to turn out the nuts onto the paper towel to cool. Makes 1⅔ cups (400 mL).

A sweet mix. You'll be popular if you share this with your friends.

Summertime Snack Mix

GET READY ✔
dry measures, large microwave-safe bowl, mixing spoon, measuring spoons, liquid measures, small bowl, oven mitts, hot pad

1.	Honey graham cereal squares	2 cups	500 mL
	"O"-shaped toasted oat cereal	2 cups	500 mL
	Dried banana chips	1 cup	250 mL
2.	Hard margarine, melted	3 tbsp.	50 mL
	Liquid honey	¼ cup	60 mL
	Ground cinnamon	½ tsp.	2 mL
	Lemon juice	2 tsp.	10 mL
3.	Chopped dried pineapple	1 cup	250 mL
	Light raisins	1 cup	250 mL
	Long thread coconut	1 cup	250 mL
	Popped corn (pop about 2 tbsp., 30 mL, kernels)	4 cups	1 L

1. Combine the first 3 ingredients with the mixing spoon in the large bowl.

2. Combine the melted margarine, honey, cinnamon and lemon juice in the small bowl. Stir. Pour the honey mixture slowly over the cereal mixture. Stir until well coated. Microwave, uncovered, on high (100%) for 2 minutes. Stir well. Microwave on high (100%) for 2 to 3 minutes, stirring at the end of each minute and watching so it does not burn. It should look toasted when done. Use the oven mitts to remove the bowl to the hot pad.

3. Add the pineapple, raisins, coconut and popcorn. Toss well. Let cool for about 1 hour. Makes 10 cups (2.5 L) snack mix.

Toasted Granola

GET READY ✔
dry measures, large bowl, long-handled mixing spoon, liquid measures, measuring spoons, 9 × 13 inch (22 × 33 cm) oblong baking pan, oven mitts, wire rack

1.			
	Large flake rolled oats (old-fashioned)	2 cups	500 mL
	Medium coconut	½ cup	125 mL
	Shelled roasted sunflower seeds	¼ cup	60 mL
	Finely chopped dried apricots	½ cup	125 mL
	Light raisins	½ cup	125 mL
	Bran flakes cereal, crushed	½ cup	125 mL
	Brown sugar, packed	⅓ cup	75 mL
2.	Cooking oil	¼ cup	60 mL
	Water	2 tbsp.	30 mL
	Vanilla (or almond) flavoring	1 tsp.	5 mL

1. Place the oven rack in the center position. Turn the oven on to 300°F (150°C). Combine the first 7 ingredients with the mixing spoon in the bowl.

2. Combine the cooking oil, water and vanilla in a liquid measure. Stir. Pour the cooking oil mixture over the granola mixture. Stir well. Spread the granola mixture in the ungreased pan. Bake in the oven for 25 minutes, stirring frequently. Use the oven mitts to remove the pan to the wire rack. Cool. Makes 5 cups (1.25 L) snack mix.

Add any chopped dried fruits in place of the apricots and raisins.

Candied Popcorn

GET READY ✔
dry measures, measuring spoons, very large bowl, 2 long-handled mixing spoons, large microwave-safe bowl, waxed paper

1.	**Popped corn (pop about ⅓ cup, 75 mL, kernels)**	10 cups	2.5 L
	Corn flakes cereal	2 cups	500 mL
	Hard margarine, melted	2 tbsp.	30 mL
2.	**Raspberry drink mix**	¼ cup	60 mL
3.	**Hard margarine**	2 tbsp.	30 mL
	Large marshmallows	36	36
	Vanilla flavoring	1 tsp.	5 mL

1. Combine the popped corn, cereal and first amount of margarine with 1 of the mixing spoons in the very large bowl. Mix well.

2. Sprinkle the drink mix over the popcorn mixture. Stir until well coated.

3. Put the second amount of margarine and marshmallows into the microwave-safe bowl. Microwave on high (100%) for 1½ to 2 minutes. Stir until the marshmallows are melted. Add the vanilla. Stir. Grease both of the mixing spoons. Pour the hot marshmallow mixture over the popcorn mixture. Toss quickly with the greased spoons until lightly coated. Lay the waxed paper on the counter or working surface. Turn the popcorn mixture out onto the waxed paper. Separate into serving-size pieces. Let cool on the waxed paper for 30 minutes. Makes 13 cups (3.25 L) popcorn mix.

A sticky situation—but worth it!

Just a hint of peanut butter and sweetness.

Peanut Butter Popcorn Treats

GET READY ✔
dry measures, small saucepan, liquid measures, mixing spoon, hot pad, measuring spoons, large bowl, baking sheet, oven mitts, wire rack

1.	**Margarine**	¼ cup	60 mL
2.	**Brown sugar, packed**	½ cup	125 mL
	Corn syrup	⅔ cup	150 mL
3.	**Smooth peanut butter**	½ cup	125 mL
	Vanilla flavoring	1 tsp.	5 mL
4.	**Popped corn (pop about ¼ cup, 60 mL, kernels)**	8 cups	2 L

1. Place the oven rack in the center position. Turn the oven on to 350°F (175°C). Melt the margarine in the saucepan on medium.

2. Add the brown sugar and corn syrup. Heat, stirring constantly with the mixing spoon, until the brown sugar is dissolved.

3. Stir in the peanut butter. Bring the mixture to a boil. Remove the saucepan to the hot pad. Stir in the vanilla flavoring.

4. Put the popcorn into the bowl. Pour the margarine mixture over the popcorn. Toss until well coated. Spread evenly on the ungreased baking sheet. Bake in the oven for 7 minutes. Use the oven mitts to remove the baking sheet to the wire rack. Cool. Break up the cooled popcorn into bite-size chunks. Makes 8 cups (2 L) popcorn mix.

CHOCO-PEANUT BUTTER POPCORN BALLS: Add 2 tbsp. (30 mL) cocoa powder along with the peanut butter to the dissolved brown sugar mixture in the saucepan. Bring to a boil. Remove the saucepan to the hot pad. Add the vanilla flavoring. Pour over the popcorn. Toss until well coated. Cool the popcorn mixture long enough so that you can handle it. Grease your hands. Shape the popcorn mixture into tennis-size balls. Place on the waxed paper to set. Makes about 14 balls.

Apricot Logs

GET READY ✔

dry measures, measuring spoons, medium microwave-safe casserole dish, blender, medium bowl, mixing spoon, waxed paper, plastic wrap, sharp knife, cutting board

1.	Dried apricots (about 40)	1½ cups	375 mL
	Water	1 tbsp.	15 mL
	Juice of 1 medium orange		
2.	Grated peel of 1 medium orange		
	Flake coconut	½ cup	125 mL
3.	Flake coconut	⅔ cup	150 mL

1. Measure the apricots and water into the casserole dish. Cover. Microwave on high (100%) for 2 minutes until moist and plump. Put the apricot mixture and orange juice into the blender. Place the lid on the blender. Process, stopping the blender and stirring every few seconds, until the apricots are very finely chopped. Put the apricot mixture into the bowl.

2. Mix in the orange peel and first amount of coconut. Divide the mixture in half. Roll into two 6 inch (15 cm) logs.

3. Place the second amount of coconut on the waxed paper. Roll the logs in the coconut until well coated. Cover each log with plastic wrap. Chill. Cut with the knife into 1 inch (2.5 cm) pieces on the cutting board. Makes 2 logs.

Pure and natural. All fruit and coconut.

Variation: Shape the mixture into 1 inch (2.5 cm) balls. Roll in the coconut. Chill. Makes about 18 balls.

Citrus Crunchies

GET READY ✔

measuring spoons, microwave-safe cup, dry measures, large bowl, mixing spoon

1.	**Margarine**	**2 tbsp.**	**30 mL**
2.	**Rice squares cereal**	**3 cups**	**750 mL**
	Package of lime, orange or grape-flavored gelatin (jelly powder), about 3 tbsp., 50 mL	**½ × 3 oz.**	**½ × 85 g**

1. Microwave the margarine in the cup on high (100%) for 20 to 30 seconds until melted.

2. Measure the cereal into the bowl. Pour the melted margarine over the cereal. Toss with the mixing spoon until well coated. Sprinkle with the flavored gelatin. Toss well. Microwave on high (100%) for 1 minute. Stir. Repeat 3 times. Makes 3 cups (750 mL) snack mix.

Great to have on hand for your lunch bag or as a dessert snack.

Corn Flakes Chews

GET READY ✔
liquid measures, large saucepan, long-handled mixing spoon, hot pad, measuring spoons, dry measures, waxed paper

1.			
	Liquid honey	¼ cup	60 mL
	Corn syrup	⅔ cup	150 mL
	Skim evaporated milk	¼ cup	60 mL
2.	Vanilla flavoring	1 tsp.	5 mL
	Corn flakes cereal	4 cups	1 L
	Fancy flake coconut	½ cup	125 mL

1. Combine the honey, corn syrup and evaporated milk in the saucepan. Heat on medium, stirring constantly with the mixing spoon, until the mixture starts to boil. Reduce the heat to medium-low. Simmer for 8 minutes. Do not stir. Remove the saucepan to the hot pad.

2. Add the vanilla, cereal and coconut. Mix well. Cool for 10 minutes. Drop by rounded tablespoonfuls onto the waxed paper. Grease your fingers. Shape into mounds. Chill for 30 minutes. Makes 24 chews.

Keep these chilled with your frozen drink box or lunch bag-size freezer pack —unless you like 'em sticky.

Banana Raisin Bars

GET READY ✔
9 x 13 inch (22 x 33 cm) oblong baking pan, dry measures, large bowl, mixing spoon, measuring spoons, small bowl, electric mixer, oven mitts, wire rack

1.	Quick-cooking rolled oats (not instant)	3 cups	750 mL
	Long thread coconut	1 cup	250 mL
	Raisins	1 cup	250 mL
	Sunflower seeds	½ cup	125 mL
	Peanuts, chopped	½ cup	125 mL
2.	Margarine	½ cup	125 mL
	Corn syrup	3 tbsp.	50 mL
	Liquid honey	3 tbsp.	50 mL
	Large egg	1	1
	Vanilla flavoring	1 tsp.	5 mL
	Mashed banana	⅓ cup	75 mL

1. Place the oven rack in the center position. Turn the oven on to 325°F (160°C). Grease the baking pan. Combine the first 5 ingredients with the mixing spoon in the large bowl.

2. Beat the next 6 ingredients in the small bowl with the electric mixer on high speed until light and fluffy. Add the banana mixture to the rolled oat mixture. Combine well. Spread in the baking pan. Press down well with your hand. Bake in the oven for 50 minutes until firm and golden brown. Use the oven mitts to remove the baking pan to the wire rack. Cool. Cuts into 36 bars.

Variation: Substitute ½ cup (125 mL) applesauce for the banana and add ⅛ tsp. (0.5 mL) ground cinnamon.

Soft and chewy. These will remind you of banana bread.

60 Squares

Sweet Ending Pizza

GET READY ✔
12 inch (30 cm) pizza pan, dry measures, large bowl, electric mixer, measuring spoons, mixing spoon, oven mitts, hot pad, table knife

1.	Smooth peanut butter	¾ cup	175 mL
	Hard margarine, softened	½ cup	125 mL
	Brown sugar, packed	1 cup	250 mL
	Granulated sugar	¼ cup	60 mL
	Large eggs	2	2
	Vanilla flavoring	1 tsp.	5 mL
2.	All-purpose flour	1¾ cups	425 mL
	Baking soda	¾ tsp.	4 mL
	Baking powder	½ tsp.	2 mL
	Salt	½ tsp.	2 mL
3.	Semisweet chocolate chips	½ cup	125 mL
	Butterscotch chips	½ cup	125 mL
4.	Candy-coated chocolate candies	½ cup	125 mL

1. Place the oven rack in the center position. Turn the oven on to 350°F (175°C). Grease the pizza pan. Cream the peanut butter and margarine together in the bowl with the electric mixer. Beat in both sugars. Beat in the eggs, 1 at a time. Add the vanilla. Stir with the mixing spoon.

2. Add the flour, baking soda, baking powder and salt. Stir just to moisten. Press in the pizza pan with your hand. Bake in the oven for 7 to 9 minutes until lightly browned. Use the oven mitts to remove the pan to the hot pad.

3. Sprinkle the hot pizza with both kinds of chips. Let stand to soften. Draw the knife back and forth to smooth out most of the chips.

4. Scatter the candies over the top of the chips. Lightly press the candies into the melted chips. Cool. Cuts into 16 wedges.

Top: Crispy Rice Squares, this page; Center: Simple Chocolate Fudge, page 63; Bottom: Butterscotch Bites, page 63.

Crispy Rice Squares

GET READY ✔
8 × 8 inch (20 × 20 cm) square baking pan, dry measures, large microwave-safe bowl, mixing spoon, 1 quart (1 L) casserole dish, table knife

1.	**Large marshmallows**	**32**	**32**
	Hard margarine	**¼ cup**	**60 mL**
2.	**Crisp rice cereal**	**5 cups**	**1.25 L**
3.	**CHOCOLATE PEANUT ICING**		
	Semisweet chocolate chips	**1 cup**	**250 mL**
	Smooth peanut butter	**¼ cup**	**60 mL**

1. Grease the baking pan. Put the marshmallows and margarine into the bowl. Microwave, uncovered, on high (100%) for about 2 minutes, stirring with the mixing spoon after 1 minute, until melted.

2. Add the cereal. Stir until well coated. Press in the pan with your hand. Cool until set.

3. **Chocolate Peanut Icing:** Put the chocolate chips and peanut butter into the casserole. Microwave, uncovered, on medium (50%) for about 2½ minutes, stirring at half-time, until melted and smooth. Spread with the knife on the squares. Cool until set. Cuts into 25 squares.

Simple Chocolate Fudge

GET READY ✔
8 × 8 inch (20 × 20 cm) square baking pan, dry measures, large microwave-safe bowl, mixing spoon

1.	Can of sweetened condensed milk	11 oz.	300 mL
	Semisweet chocolate chips	3 cups	750 mL
2.	Chopped walnuts	⅔ cup	150 mL

1. Grease the baking pan. Put the condensed milk and chocolate chips into the bowl. Microwave, uncovered, on medium (50%) for about 2½ minutes, stirring often with the mixing spoon, until the chips are melted.

2. Add the walnuts. Stir. Spread in the pan. Chill. Cuts into 25 squares.

Pictured on page 62.

Butterscotch Bites

GET READY ✔
dry measures, liquid measures, large deep microwave-safe bowl, mixing spoon, baking sheet, waxed paper

1.	Granulated sugar	¾ cup	175 mL
	Hard margarine	¼ cup	60 mL
	Skim evaporated milk	⅓ cup	75 mL
2.	Butterscotch chips	½ cup	125 mL
3.	Quick-cooking rolled oats (not instant)	1¾ cups	425 mL
	Medium coconut	¼ cup	60 mL

1. Combine the sugar, margarine and evaporated milk with the mixing spoon in the bowl. Microwave, uncovered, on high (100%) for about 2 minutes until the mixture boils. Stir. Microwave on medium (50%) for 1 minute.

2. Add the chips. Stir until melted.

3. Mix in the rolled oats and coconut. Cover the baking sheet with the waxed paper. Drop the mixture by rounded tablespoonfuls onto the waxed paper. Chill until firm. Keep chilled. Makes about 2 dozen bites.

Pictured on page 62.

Your mouth will water for these.

Chocolate Chip Granola Bars

GET READY ✓
10 × 15 inch (25 × 38 cm) baking sheet, dry measures, liquid measures, large bowl, mixing spoon, waxed paper, oven mitts, wire rack

1.			
Rolled oats (not instant)	3 cups	750 mL
Flaked almonds	1 cup	250 mL
Shelled sunflower seeds	1 cup	250 mL
Raisins	1 cup	250 mL
Semisweet chocolate chips	1 cup	250 mL
Can of sweetened condensed milk	11 oz.	300 mL
Hard margarine, melted	¼ cup	60 mL

1. Place the oven rack in the center position. Turn the oven on to 325°F (160°C). Grease the baking sheet. Combine all 7 ingredients with the mixing spoon in the bowl. The mixture will be stiff. Put into the baking sheet. Press down evenly with your hands using the waxed paper. Bake in the oven for 25 to 30 minutes until golden brown. Use the oven mitts to remove the baking sheet to the wire rack. Cool for 15 minutes. Cuts into 36 bars.

64 Squares

Great any time of the day.

Puffed Wheat Candy Squares

GET READY ✔

dry measures, large bowl, 9 × 13 inch (22 × 33 cm) oblong baking pan, medium saucepan, liquid measures, measuring spoons, long-handled mixing spoon, hot pad

1.	Puffed wheat cereal	8 cups	2 L
2.	Hard margarine	⅓ cup	75 mL
	Golden corn syrup	½ cup	125 mL
	Liquid honey	1 tsp.	5 mL
	Smooth peanut butter	1½ tbsp.	25 mL
	Brown sugar, packed	1 cup	250 mL
3.	Vanilla flavoring	1 tsp.	5 mL
4.	Hard margarine	½ tsp.	2 mL

1. Measure the cereal into the bowl. Grease the pan.

2. Melt the first amount of margarine in the saucepan on medium. Add the corn syrup, honey, peanut butter and brown sugar. Heat on medium, stirring constantly with the mixing spoon, until the mixture comes to a boil and the brown sugar is dissolved. This should take about 30 to 40 seconds. Remove the saucepan to the hot pad.

3. Add the vanilla. Stir. Carefully pour the sauce over the cereal. Stir until the cereal is well coated. Put the cereal mixture into the pan.

4. Grease the palms of your hands with the second amount of margarine. Press the cereal mixture with your hand into the pan. Cool until set. Cuts into 48 squares.

Puffed Wheat Squares

GET READY ✔
9 × 9 inch (22 × 22 cm) square baking pan, dry measures, measuring spoons, medium saucepan, mixing spoon, hot pad, very large bowl, rubber spatula

1.			
	Hard margarine	⅓ cup	75 mL
	Light or dark corn syrup	½ cup	125 mL
	Brown sugar, packed	⅔ cup	150 mL
	Cocoa powder	2 tbsp.	30 mL
	Vanilla flavoring	1 tsp.	5 mL
2.	Puffed wheat cereal	8 cups	2 L

1. Grease the baking pan. Combine the margarine, corn syrup, brown sugar, cocoa powder and vanilla flavoring with the mixing spoon in the saucepan. Heat on medium, stirring constantly, until the mixture starts to boil with bubbles all over the surface. Remove the saucepan to the hot pad.

2. Measure the cereal into the bowl. Pour the hot chocolate mixture over the top. Use the rubber spatula to scrape the sides of the saucepan. Stir until well coated. Turn into the pan. Press down using the dampened spatula. Chill for about 2 hours to set. Cuts into 36 squares.

Pictured on page 67.

Rice Crispy Squares

GET READY ✔
9 × 9 inch (22 × 22 cm) square baking pan, dry measures, large saucepan (or Dutch oven), mixing spoon, hot pad, rubber spatula

1.	Hard margarine	¼ cup	60 mL
	Large marshmallows	36	36
2.	Crisp rice cereal	6 cups	1.5 L

1. Grease the pan. Put the margarine and marshmallows into the saucepan. Heat on medium, stirring often with the mixing spoon, until melted. Remove the saucepan to the hot pad.

2. Add the cereal. Stir until well coated. Scrape out all of the cereal into the pan. Press down firmly using the dampened rubber spatula. Chill for about 2 hours before cutting. Cuts into 36 squares.

Pick one of these guaranteed favorites. Puffed Wheat Squares, page 66, are pictured on the left. Rice Crispy Squares, above, are shown on the right.

Very easy and quick to make. Spread as much liverwurst on the tortilla as you like.

"Wurst" Cheese & Lettuce Wrap

GET READY ✔

measuring spoons, table knife, dry measures, plastic wrap

1.			
Plain (or herbed) liverwurst		2-3 tbsp.	30-50 mL
White (or whole wheat) flour tortilla (10 inch, 25 cm, size)		1	1
Grated Swiss cheese		⅓ cup	75 mL
Shredded lettuce		⅓-½ cup	75-125 mL

1. Spread the liverwurst with the knife on the tortilla. Sprinkle with the cheese and lettuce. Roll up tightly. Wrap with plastic wrap. Chill for at least 1 hour. Makes 1 wrap.

Vegetable Roll

GET READY ✔
measuring spoons, small bowl, mixing spoon, table knife, dry measures,
plastic wrap

1.	Plain spreadable cream cheese	1 tbsp.	15 mL
	Ranch (or other creamy) dressing	1 tbsp.	15 mL
	White (or whole wheat) flour tortilla (10 inch, 25 cm, size)	1	1
2.	Grated carrot	2 tbsp.	30 mL
	Finely chopped green, red or yellow pepper	2 tbsp.	30 mL
	Finely chopped green onion	2 tsp.	10 mL
	Finely chopped broccoli florets	3 tbsp.	50 mL
	Grated Cheddar cheese	¼ cup	60 mL

1. Combine the cream cheese and dressing with the mixing spoon in the bowl. Spread the cream cheese mixture with the knife on the tortilla.

2. Sprinkle the remaining 5 ingredients on the cream cheese mixture in the order given. Roll up tightly. Wrap with plastic wrap. Chill for at least 1 hour. Makes 1 roll.

Try different flavored dressings for a variety of tastes.

Roast Beef Rolls

GET READY ✓

measuring spoons, table knife, dry measures, plastic wrap

1.			
Plain (or herbed) spreadable cream cheese	3 tbsp.	50 mL
White (or whole wheat) flour tortilla (10 inch, 25 cm, size)	1	1
Shredded lettuce	½ cup	125 mL
Finely diced onion	1 tbsp.	15 mL
Shaved roast beef (or 3 very thin slices)	2 oz.	57 g

1. Spread the cream cheese with the knife on the tortilla. Cover with the lettuce and onion. Lay the beef on top. Roll up tightly. Wrap with plastic wrap. Chill for at least 1 hour. Makes 1 roll. Slice to serve.

Try dipped in Honey Mustard Dunk, page 23.

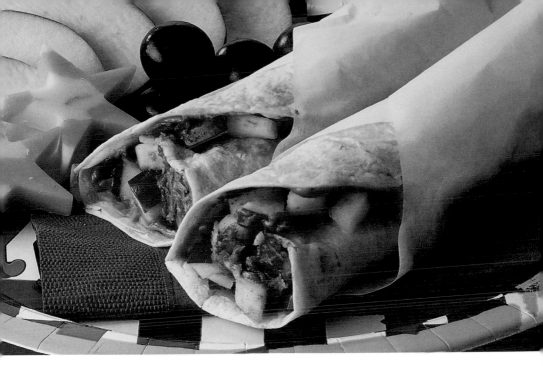

Much more fun than your ordinary peanut butter sandwich.

Peanut Butter Wrap

GET READY ✔

measuring spoons, table knife, dry measures, small cup, table spoon, plastic wrap

1.	Peanut butter	2 tbsp.	30 mL
	White (or whole wheat) flour tortilla (10 inch, 25 cm, size)	1	1
	Chopped apple, with peel	½ cup	125 mL
2.	Brown sugar, packed	1 tsp.	5 mL
	Ground cinnamon	¼ tsp.	1 mL

1. Spread the peanut butter with the knife on the tortilla. Scatter the apple on the peanut butter.

2. Combine the brown sugar and cinnamon with the spoon in the cup. Sprinkle over the apple. Roll up tightly. Wrap with plastic wrap. Chill for at least 1 hour. Makes 1 wrap.

Pack these for your lunch. Easy to eat.

Cucumber Under Wraps

GET READY ✔

measuring spoons, table knife, plastic wrap

1.	Plain (or herbed) spreadable cream cheese	½ cup	125 mL
	White (or whole wheat) flour tortillas (8 inch, 20 cm, size)	4	4
2.	Cucumber piece (6 inches, 15 cm, long), quartered lengthwise	1	1
	Salt, sprinkle (optional)		
	Pepper, sprinkle (optional)		

1. Spread 2 tbsp. (30 mL) cream cheese with the knife on each tortilla.

2. Lay 1 cucumber spear on 1 edge of each tortilla. Sprinkle with the salt and pepper. Roll each tortilla around the cucumber. Wrap tightly with plastic wrap. Chill for at least 1 hour. Makes 4 wraps.

Measurement Tables

Throughout this book measurements are given in Conventional and Metric measures. The tables below provide a quick reference for the standard measures, weights, temperatures, and sizes.

Spoons

Conventional Measure	Metric Standard Measure Millilitre (mL)
1/8 teaspoon (tsp.)	0.5 mL
1/4 teaspoon (tsp.)	1 mL
1/2 teaspoon (tsp.)	2 mL
1 teaspoon (tsp.)	5 mL
2 teaspoons (tsp.)	10 mL
1 tablespoon (tbsp.)	15 mL

Cups

Conventional Measure	Metric Standard Measure Millilitre (mL)
1/4 cup (4 tbsp.)	60 mL
1/3 cup (5 tbsp.)	75 mL
1/2 cup (8 tbsp.)	125 mL
2/3 cup (10 tbsp.)	150 mL
3/4 cup (12 tbsp.)	175 mL
1 cup (16 tbsp.)	250 mL
4 cups	1000 mL(1 L)

Weights

Ounces (oz.)	Grams (g)
1 oz.	28 g
2 oz.	57 g
3 oz.	85 g
4 oz.	113 g
5 oz.	140 g
6 oz.	170 g
7 oz.	200 g
8 oz.	225 g
16 oz. (1 lb.)	454 g
32 oz. (2 lbs.)	900 g
35 oz. (2.2 lbs.)	1000 g (1 kg)

Oven Temperature

Fahrenheit (°F)	Celsius (°C)
175°	80°
200°	95°
225°	110°
250°	120°
275°	140°
300°	150°
325°	160°
350°	175°
375°	190°
400°	205°
425°	220°
450°	230°
475°	240°
500°	260°

Pans

Conventional Inches	Metric Centimetres
8x8 inch	20x20 cm
9x9 inch	22x22 cm
9x13 inch	22x33 cm
10x15 inch	25x38 cm
11x17 inch	28x43 cm
8x2 inch round	20x5 cm
9x2 inch round	22x5 cm
10x4 1/2 inch tube	25x11 cm
8x4x3 inch loaf	20x10x7.5 cm
9x5x3 inch loaf	22x12.5x7.5 cm

Casseroles

Conventional Quart (qt.)	Metric Litre (L)
1 qt.	1 L
1 1/2 qt.	1.5 L
2 qt.	2 L
2 1/2 qt.	2.5 L
3 qt.	3 L
4 qt.	4 L

 Index

Feature Recipe from

Weekend Treats

Having a sleep-over? Watching videos with a friend? Thinking about food? Weekend Treats is for you!

Snowballs

GET READY ✔

dry measures, large saucepan, liquid measures, measuring spoons, long-handled mixing spoon, hot pad, small bowl, waxed paper, covered container

1.	Hard margarine	½ cup	125 mL
	Chopped pitted dates	2 cups	500 mL
	Water	¼ cup	60 mL
	Ground cinnamon	⅛ tsp.	0.5 mL
2.	Chopped walnuts (or pecans), optional	½ cup	125 mL
	Granola cereal	½ cup	125 mL
	Crisp rice cereal	⅓ cup	125 mL
3.	Flake coconut	¾ cup	175 mL

1. Melt the margarine in the saucepan on medium. Add the dates, water and cinnamon. Stir. Heat until the mixture comes to a boil. Turn down the heat to low. Heat, stirring constantly, for 5 minutes until the mixture is thickened. Remove the saucepan to the hot pad. Cool for 10 minutes.

2. Add the walnuts, granola cereal and rice cereal. Mix well.

3. Put the coconut into the small bowl. Wet your hands with water. Shape the cereal mixture into 1 inch (2.5 cm) balls. Roll the balls in the coconut. Place on the waxed paper on the counter or chill in a covered container. Serve at room temperature or chilled. Makes 30 balls.

Cook's Notes